C000193601

How to Create A WordPress Blog Step By Step In 2019

Learn How to Setup A WordPress Blog. Discover Profitable Blogging Ideas with Low Competition

Paul O. Garten

How to Create A Wordpress Blog Step By Step In 2019

Learn How to Setup A WordPress Blog. Discover Profitable Blogging Ideas with Low Competition

Paul O. Garten

Copyright © June 2019

Contents

Introduction

Blogging has continued to evolve over the years and has become a stable source of income for families. Many have invested their time, money, and other resources into blogging and have reaped bountifully from their investment while others have had their investment in blogging going down the drain, and their blogging career got buried. I'm writing to you today because I've been there; I've tasted what it means for a blog to fail, not once or twice, but at every point I knew the time was up, I said to myself, "Maybe I'd have to try again." I read some good stuff according to the gurus, but when I apply to my blog, I got a different result: many times discouraging and few times quite encouraging.

I learned my lesson, and finally, I got to a bliss point: a good blogging idea or niche, and content are all that matters. Once I got those two rights, my ranking and traffic automatically picked up even with few articles on the blog. As a blogger, you have to write first for Search Engines before humans in the right niche. Succeeding on blogging largely depends on technicalities and not necessarily on the general knowledge every aspiring blogger has about blogging. You may have money to invest and scale things up, but without the right knowledge, all your dollars won't yield any results. You must have at least 70% of the required knowledge while you can pay for, outsource or buy the remaining 30%. Apart from blogging, don't go into any business you don't know at least 70% about it. You may likely fail at it. Knowledge is power—far more powerful than just money.

Mindset Re-Orientation

Blogging is a journey, and that journey begins with your mind. You must have the right mindset about blogging else you will fail. Every day, thousands of domains expire, and the connected blogs hit the rock of disappointment. The owners of those domains at one time had hopes of making thousands of dollars, if not millions from blogging but along the line, things changed, and they parked off.

Now, I don't want you to get this book as a way of getting started with blogging, and later you dropped the idea—probably after reading to the end, and beginning to acquire the necessary things and suddenly, you realize that blogging isn't for you. No! Make up your mind right now if this is something you want to do. You must have read or heard stories of people about how profitable blogging is, and you got carried away and choose to blog too. Well, you've not gone far, you can change your mind now instead of wasting your time and resources starting a blog and later you back out.

Blogging is profitable but could be tough to break even. It doesn't even depend on if you have money to spend and force things to work. If you think you will be able to hold on until you get to that level, you'd begin to depend on your blog for everything then go ahead. You can create a successful blog. Blogging isn't rocket science; after all, that's why you're buying this book.

Inside this book, you would learn how to take off as a beginner to a professional in blogging. One thing that usually frustrates beginners is search engine optimization – this book has done justice to that. You will also find some important recommended plugins for your blog. For the most part, you won't have to buy or pay for anything again after the initial spending you do to set up your blog. Do most things yourself so that you can understand the nitty-gritty of the art. Soil your hands with the art of blogging.

Having the beginner blogger in mind, the book uses image illustrations to explain things where necessary so that you can get the message in it loud and clear. We believe beyond doubt that you will succeed with this guide in your journey to building a successful blog that you can depend on to pay your bills.

Lastly, have in mind that the journey of a thousand miles begins with a bold step. You've taken a step in that journey to buy this book; next, get into the ring and fight. Life is a fight. Do the right things always. Prepare your mind to sit for long hours to write and publish quality contents. Try to write most of your articles except you can find good writers. What many of them does is spin articles and force it to pass plagiarism check.

1 ➤ WordPress.org vs. WordPress.com

WordPress is a web-based application available on https://WordPress.org which can be used to create great blogs or websites. WordPress is open-source software, which means that you can download it and use it as you wish. In summary, WordPress.org hosts the WordPress software that anybody can download, install on their web host and use as their blogging platform.

WordPress.org also plays host to thousands of plugins or add-ons for its WordPress software. WordPress.com, on the other hand, is a commercial website similar to Blogger.com. It hosts the WordPress software for creating blogs but with a limited manipulative ability of the user. Now you have options to choose between the WordPress software with a web host where you can customize it as desire or WordPress.com where you can even create a free blog on it, but with your ability to customize your blog being limited to what the platform has to offer. Where the former, when implemented, can be referred to as a self-hosted WordPress blog, the latter can be referred to as a pre-hosted WordPress blog.

What are the pros and cons of one over the other?

With a self-hosted WordPress, you have complete control over your blog, and you are free to do what you want to do with it. No one's giving you terms and conditions on how to use their blog platform. You are free to install/uninstall any theme, or plug-in. You can also edit the code of your theme, plug-in or even the WordPress software as you want. However, for a pre-hosted WordPress blog, these functionalities are limited, but it's far easier to set up and maintain.

All you need to do to set up a pre-hosted blog is to visit the WordPress.com website and then click on the **Start Your Website** link to begin setting up your blog. Next, enter your website URL and choose your blog theme, and within seconds, your blog is up and running. Unfortunately, you'll have to make do with your blog ending with .WordPress.com. To change the

.WordPress.com to just .com, you will have to buy a custom domain name from WordPress.com or any third-party domain name registrar then transfer it to WordPress.com. This may involve charges. Like any domain name for a self-hosted blog, you will have to renew your domain name once every year.

There are also free plugins included with a free hosted blog, but you can't install your plugin or theme. You can't also edit the WordPress code. Customization options are limited, and because you don't pay for hosting, your blog can be taken down if you violate their terms and conditions, but where you pay for hosting and have to manage everything by yourself, that can't happen. If it happens, you have every right to sue your web host.

2 ➤ Getting a Domain Name, a Theme and a Paid WordPress Hosting

Some recommendations come in handy in choosing a domain name:

- Always go for a .com domain extension.
- Easy to memorize.
- Easy to pronounce.
- Easy to remember.
- Make it brandable.
- Make it unique.
- Sounds trustworthy.
- Make it short and simple.
- Keyword targeted.
- No hyphen in-between words, e.g., baseball-fans.com.
- Don't mix it with numbers, e.g., mega360.com.
- Make it predictable from the sound.
- Don't infringe a trademark.

What more? Register your domain name with the same company that you want to play hosting to your WordPress blog and avoid unnecessary transfer of a domain name from one registrar to another.

Most places selling domain names can also play host to your WordPress blog. Go for any of such places. You can buy a domain or host your WordPress with Hostgator, Namecheap, Hover, Godaddy, Gandi, Dreamhost, Name, 1and1, Network Solutions, Flippa, Hostinger, Domain.com, Bluehost, Wix.com, Web.com, and more. You can walk around these places and see what they offer.

You can also search and buy a theme from ThemeForest or MyThemeShop for $30-$70.

3 ➤ Setting Up Your WordPress Blog

Installing WordPress

WordPress installation methods largely depend on what WordPress installation technology that your Web Host is using. We will look at two common methods here.

Method 1: Web Hosts with cPanel

Once you've paid for a domain name and hosting plan, go to your Web Host cPanel to begin your WordPress installation. Note that if you never purchased your domain name with the same Web Host, you will have to transfer it from your domain name registrar to your Web Host before you can install WordPress on it. Once you've done that launch your host's cPanel to install your WordPress by following the steps below:

- Scroll down and click on **Softaculous Apps Installer** under **Software**.

- Click on **Blog** by the left panel and then **WordPress**.

- Click **Install** and select the right domain for the installation if you have more than a domain name with your Web host.

- Under **Site Settings**, type your **Site Name** and **Site Description**.

- Under **Admin Account**, set your **Admin Username** and **Password**. Also, set your Admin E-mail (if any).

- Tick the box to limit login attempts. If doing this, don't install the Login LockDown plugin again.

- Under **Advanced Options**, tick to **Auto Upgrade WordPress, Plugins** and **Themes**.

- Click **Install**.

Congrats! You've just installed the WordPress software on your blog. Your blog is now available at **http://yourdomain.com/wp-admin** where "yourdomain.com" is your blog's domain name. Going forward, use this URL to access and login to your WordPress blog backend as the admin.

Method 2: Web Hosts without cPanel

Web hosts using the cPanel have a straight WordPress installation steps once you are on the cPanel, but for other hosts not using this method, WordPress installation is still similar. Differences only exist where they placed their option for installing the software.

Generally, make sure your host has the domain name you are installing the WordPress software for before trying to install the software. Having the two things (domain name and hosting) in place, scan through and locate the menu where you have **Apps** on your host and click on WordPress to begin the installation. **Select your domain name** and **Continue**. Once the installation is complete, your WordPress username and password is emailed to you. Basically, your WordPress username is the same username that you are using on your Web Host.

Congrats! You've just installed the WordPress software on your blog. Your new blog is now available at **http://yourdomain.com/wp-admin** where "yourdomain.com" is your blog's domain name. Going forward, use this URL to access and login to your WordPress blog backend as the admin. Once login, change your password. See *"Customizing Your WordPress Blog"* to learn more.

Other times, once you pay for a domain name and hosting plan, your host handles your WordPress installation without you lifting a finger and when the installation is complete, they email your login details to you. You can request them to install the software for you if this is what you want.

Installing Theme

It's very simple and straightforward to change your WordPress Theme from the default that comes with it after installing the software.

To get started, hover your mouse on **Appearance** and then click on **Theme**. This takes you to the WordPress Theme area where you can find both free and paid themes for your blog. Scroll down to type a keyword to bring up more themes and then hover your mouse on your preferred theme and **Install** it on your blog.

You may have downloaded a Theme and stored it in a location on your Computer. To install this theme, click on **Add New** on top of the page and then click **Upload Theme**. Next, click **Choose File** from your Computer. Click **Install Now** to begin installing your new theme. After installing the theme, hover your mouse on it to **Activate** or see a **Live Preview** of it.

To customize your Theme, hover your mouse on **Appearance** and then click on **Theme Options**.

WordPress Plugins

What are plugins? I'm pretty sure you own a smartphone, and we can use that to explain what a plugin is all about, especially as it has to do with your WordPress blogging. Now, your smartphone runs on a mobile operating system (OS) which may be Android or iOS. The mobile OS is the based or root software that enables the apps on the phone to work. If something goes wrong with the mobile's operating system, it will affect the functionality of all applications on the phone.

At any time, you can easily visit the mobile's OS app store to download apps based on what you want the app to do for you or in your phone. While conducting a search for any particular app keyword (e.g., battery saver) within the app store, lots of related apps for the keyword shows up. From there, you can check, download, install the one that resonates with you, and finally, you can find the newly installed app when you tap on the phone's main menu.

The illustration above is similar to what WordPress and its plugin are all about. In the case of a WordPress blog, the WordPress software is similar to your phone's OS while a WordPress plugin is similar to your mobile apps, but in blogging, they are referred to as plugins.

Depending on what you want a plugin to do on your WordPress blog, you search for the plugin with a [related] keyword and then look closely at the search result and install the best for your blog. After plugin installation, you must activate it to have the plugin work the way it should.

There are several plugins in the WordPress blogosphere and tens of keyword-specific plugins. You don't have the luxury of downloading any plugin into your WordPress blog for two main reasons:

(a) limited storage.

(b) conflicts with WordPress.

You already know what to do to manage your storage – deactivate or delete less functional or redundant plugins or buy more storage space from your hosting provider. However, in the case of conflict, it's better imagined than experiencing it. In your WordPress blogging journey, you will face serious temptation to download more and more plugins for your blog, but you will have to be careful to avoid WordPress plugin problems. You will have to also go for important plugins. Plugin conflicts consume a lot of time. You may have to sit and deactivate all plugins on your blog one after the other to fish out the one causing a problem. Other times, it may lead to a serious crisis that can prevent you from logging into your blog backend. Beware!

Finally, we can define blog plugins as 3rd-party add-ons responsible for specialized functions on a blog. For example, we have plugins for SEO, plugins for traffic stats, plugins for newsletter subscription, plugins for cookies, etc.

To get started with WordPress plugins for your blog,

1. Hover your mouse on **Plugins** from the left **WordPress Menu** panel to reveal the **Contextual Menu**.

On the Contextual Menu:

2. Click **Installed Plugins** to view all plugins installed on your blog.

3. Click **Add New** to add new or install a plugin on your blog.

Two methods to add a plugin to your blog include:

(a) If you've downloaded a plugin on WordPress.org or elsewhere and store it in a location on your Computer, click **Upload** to locate and install the plugin on your WordPress blog. Finally, click **Activate** to get the plugin to start working immediately.

(b) Click the **keyword box** to enter a related keyword for the nature of plugin that you want or the exact name of the plugin if you know. The system searches automatically and displays the result on the screen. Click on **Install** against the plugin to quickly install it on your blog. The system prompts for compatibility issues during installation with the version of your WordPress (if any). Finally, click **Activate** to set the plugin in motion.

Where necessary, you may be required to adjust some settings for your plugin to work. Repeat steps 1 and 2 above then locate the plugin concerned and click the **Settings** link against it to tune the **Settings** of the plugin accordingly.

Besides the **Settings** link is another link to **Deactivate**a plugin. Take note that every plugin you've installed on your blog has the **Deactivate** link against it. Click on the link if there's a need to stop a plugin from working on your blog. Deactivated plugins goes into **Inactive** (see top of the plugin page). Others include **Active** (to see all active plugins), **Update Available** (to see plugins that requires update), and **All** (to see all your plugins).

To remove/delete a plugin from your blog, go the **Installed** plugins page, click the **checkbox** against any plugin that you want to delete and then go to where you have **Bulk Actions**, click on it and select **Delete** from the options. Finally, click on **Apply** to delete the selected plugin(s).

Tips

- To download the best plugins for your blog, always read the reviews of other users of that plugin and also check the number of downloads the plugin enjoys. A higher number means that the plugin is good, while a lower number of downloads may not mean that the plugin is bad, but may indicate that the plugin is relatively new on WordPress. Take your time to read users' comments about a plugin before installing it on your blog and also check that it is compatible with the version of your version of WordPress.

- Click on **Install Plugins** from the WordPress menu by the left to see few recommended plugins.

Editing a plugin

It could be dangerous to edit a plugin as such action on a single plugin can destabilize your blog. However, if you are skilled and feel you know what you are doing, you can go ahead, but it is highly recommended you don't edit a plugin on your blog. However, to edit a plugin, repeat step 1 above and then on the **Contextual Menu**, click **Plugin editor**. You will be responsible for whatever happens to your blog after that.

Recommended Plugins for Your New Blog

Find a handful free, but effective WordPress plugins you can install to get started with your new blog. This is in addition to other plugin mentions in this book.

1. To manage your comments, install **Disqus for WordPress** by Disqus.

2. Install **Amazon send to Kindle** by Amazon.com to enable blog readers to

send your blog posts to their Kindle device and read later.

3. Install **Classic Editor**by WordPress Contributors to work with a stable WordPress editor instead of the unstable Gutenberg blocks.

4. **Search and Replace** by Delicious Brains would help you convert all http URLS to https after moving from http to https.

5. Insert a contact form automatically into your contact us page with **Contact Form 7** by Takayuki Nkyoshi.

6. Comply with the EU cookie law by installing a **Cookie Notice** plugin by dFactory.

7. The **Easy Table of Content** plugin by Steven Zahm insert an automatic table of contents into your blog post. Readers can easily click to jump to a section within the post.

8. The **Google Analytics Dashboard** by ExactMetrics shows traffic stats about your blog and related analysis.

9. If you need your blog readers to be able to rate your post, then install, activate and set up the **Rate My Post** plugin by Blaz K. This plugin is one of the best rating plugins you can find around.

10. **Schema** by Brainstorm Force is a plugin that helps search engines to understand the nature of your post and its structure.

11. **ShareThis share button** by ShareThis allows users to share your post to social media.

12. Use **Silky Custom CSS and JS** by SilkyPress.com to add custom codes to your site.

13. Host your ads.txt file from Google in your site using the **Ads.txt manager** plugin by 10up.

14. The **Simple WP Sitemap** plugin by Webbjocke would help generate a sitemap file that you can submit to Google and other search engines.

15. The **TinyMCE Advanced** plugin by Andrew Ozzadds more formatting features to your WordPress editor.

16. If you need to put off your site from visitors while working on it, then go for **Maintenance Mode** by DesignModo.

17. Install, activate, and set up the **WP Notification Bar** by MyThemeShop to post notifications to your blog readers.

18. You may choose to go with **RankMath** by MyThemeShopor **Yoast SEO** plugin for your onpage SEO needs.

19. The **Advanced WP Columns** plugin would help create columns in your blog post when you need them.

20. Use the **Simple FB** plugin and/or the **Twitter Feed** plugin to connect your site with your social media account.

4 ➤ Customizing Your WordPress Blog

The WordPress Dashboard

The WordPress dashboard is the first thing you see when you log into your Admin backend. Once there, change your password from the long auto-generated password sent to your e-mail from your web host when WordPress was first installed.

To change the default password, move your mouse over **Howdy, Admin** and then click on **Logout**. On the login page, hit **Forgot Password** and insert your e-mail address that associate with your WordPress account. Next, click on **Get New Password**. Check your e-mail to see the confirmation link. Click on the **link** to set a **new password** for your WordPress blog. Type your new password consisting of upper and lower case letters, symbols, and numbers to make it difficult for any unauthorized person that tries to log into your WordPress account. Make your password up to eight characters. Finally, click on **Reset Password**.

You can also update your WordPress software to the latest version by clicking **Please Update WordPress**. Note that if your WordPress is updated to the latest version, you won't find any WordPress update link to click.

For your plugin updates, click on **Updates**. On the ensuing page, you can update your plugins one after the other or by marking to update them in bulk.

Click on **Screen Options** to select the features you would like to see the next time you log in. We have options such as At a Glance, Activity, Google Analytics Dashboard (if the plugin is installed), Quick Draft, etc.

Click on **Help** to access more help resources.

Adjusting the Settings

Move your mouse over **Settings** from the **WordPress menu** by the left to see the contextual menu of Settings. Don't forget to click on **Save Changes** down the screen to save your new settings any time you adjust a setting.

General

Here, you can set your site title, tag line, admin e-mail, etc. Once done, scroll down and click on **Save Changes**. You don't necessarily need to touch the two URLs.

Writing

Under **Writing**, you can set your Default Post Category. After settings, you default post category, every post you publish without selecting a category for it enters here.

Post Format includes Standard, Aside, Chat, Gallery, Link, etc. You may choose to allow your blog users to switch the WordPress editor or you set a standing editor for everyone under **Default Editor**. We also have **Post via e-mail** where you can link up your blog to your e-mail to make a blog post.

Reading

Do you want your latest posts or a static page to show on your blog home page? Indicate here.

For whatever reason, you can also discourage SEs not to index your site.

Discussion

Discussion takes care of your comment settings.

Media

Leave the Media Settings as is. Set your Privacy Policy page under Privacy Settings. Once there, you can select a privacy page that you created or Create New Page.

Setting Up Your Primary Pages: Privacy Policy, Contact and About Us

Once you are through with installing the WordPress software on your hosting, creating and setting up your primary pages is next in line.

To begin, create your privacy policy and about us pages following the standard method of creating pages in WordPress. See *"Creating, Editing or Deleting a WordPress Page"* on how to create pages. You can easily search for samples of a privacy policy on the web and edit it accordingly to suit your needs capturing essentially what user data you collect on your site and how you intend to use the data. For "About Us," simply write about yourself as the admin/owner of the blog and what the blog is all about.

To create a contact page, see *"WordPress Plugins"* on how to download and install a plugin. Search for and install the plugin, **Contact Form 7** before creating a contact page. Now, what Contact Form 7 does is to automatically insert a simple contact form into a page where your blog readers can use to get in touch with you. Do just that and create your contact page.

Once you are through with creating and publishing all these pages, it's time to position them. Get their links and get set to position them where they should appear. While some Webmasters prefer to keep the privacy policy page in the footer and the other pages in the header, other prefers keeping all in the header. It's up to you, but I prefer the former.

To access your blog footer, hover your mouse on **Appearance** from the **WordPress menu**, click on **Theme Options** and then **Footer**. In the Copyright text box, type something like: `<a href="https://example.com/privacy-policy/" rel="nofollow">Privacy Policy</a>`. Replace the URL with that of your privacy policy page. Finally, click on **Save Changes** to save what you've done.

For the Contact and About Us pages, see *"Creating a Navigational Menu in Wordpress"* on how to link your pages to the header bar.

5 ➤ Adding A User and Creating a Role for Your Blog Users

You may choose to allow others to post contents to your blog or respond to comments from readers. Depending on what you want the user to do, you can assign them a role. This section of the book explains how you can go about that.

How to add a user

To add a user, move your mouse over **Users** and then click **Add New User**. Fill the required details and set the user **Role**. Click **Add New User** to create their profile.

How to remove or change a user role

To remove or change user role, click on **All Users**. Click on the checkbox to mark a user and then click on **Bulk Actions**, select **Delete**, and finally click on **Apply** to effect the selected option on the user. You can also click on **Change Role to...** to select a new role for the user and then click **Change** to save your changes.

6 ➤WordPress Blog Security Implementation

Making Your Site Hack-Proof

You may not really have a problem with hackers when you are just starting, but once your site begins to gain momentum, it attracts hackers so you'd have to prepare for them. Make sure you implement the following measures to make your site hack-proof.

Set a strong password

This step can't be over-emphasized. Your WordPress password must be strong in such a way that no one can guess it. Make your password a combination of uppercase and lowercase letters, symbols, numbers and even with white space bar. Make it up to eight characters. See *"Customizing Your WordPress Blog"* to learn more.

Don't store your WordPress passwords on your browser

Don't permit your browser to save your password on the system such that once you launch the WordPress site, you only have to click login without entering the password again. No! Enter your login details every time you want to access your browser's backend.

Password your Computer

If you have to login credentials on your Web browser, then you have to password your Computer, but what if your Computer's password is broken? Hence, go with option (2) above.

Keep your WordPress software updated

Make sure your WordPress blog is kept updated. See *"The WordPress Dashboard"* under *"Customizing Your WordPress Blog"* to learn more.

Keep your Theme and Plugins updated

Update your theme and plugins. See *"The WordPress Dashboard"* under

"Customizing Your WordPress Blog" to learn more.

Keep your WordPress version number hidden

Download, install, and activate the **Remove** plugin. The **Remove** plugin removes or hides your WordPress version number from hackers. If they know your WordPress version, they can easily work around to get a specific hacking strategy for your WordPress version, but keeping this number away from them make their work of breaking into your backend a bit difficult.

Keep track of who logs into your blog

Download, install, and activate the **Simple Login Log**. The plugin helps keep track of IP addresses that logs into your WordPress blog. This is especially useful if you have more people working on your site under different roles.

Stop repeated login attempts

Download, install and activate **Login LockDown** plugin to stop brute force attacks on your site. It stops someone that repeatedly tries to gain entry into your backend.

Implement a two-step security on your login

Download, install and activate **Google Authenticator** to implement a two-step security on your login. The Amazon website is a perfect example for this where the system sometimes would e-mail you a code to insert before you can continue logging into the site, especially when the system detects IP or location change.

Watch your network

Don't connect to an unsecured Wi-Fi network where someone can easily intercept your data packets and monitor your online activities. Make sure that any Wi-Fi network that you want to connect to has the key lock sign against it.

Keep viruses away from your Computer

Make sure your system doesn't have viruses on it. You can download and install AVG or Avast free Antivirus to keep your system safe.

Mind your uploads

Make sure you do all your media uploads by yourself and from your system.

Moving from the Unsecured HTTP to a Secured HTTPS

Some websites are offering the SSL service such as Let's Encrypt, Cloudflare, Comodo, etc. but we'll be using Cloudflare to demonstrate how you can move your site from the unsecured HTTP protocol to a secure https protocol. This step is particularly important because Google mostly ranks only secured site with SSL implemented on it.

To get started, follow the steps below:

1. Visit cloudflare.com.
2. Sign up, add your site, and click **Next**.
3. Choose the free plan and **Confirm Plan**.

4. Scroll down and click **Continue**.
5. Go to your domain name registrar's site and log in to access domain name. The dashboard should display all your domain names.
6. Click **Manage** against the domain name that you want to point to Cloudflare.
7. Change your DNS records (DNS 1 and 2) to reflect those of Cloudflare. Add records as **Custom DNS** and **Save**.
8. Click on **Continue** on Cloudflare.
9. Fetch your site from Cloudflare and give 24hrs for changes to propagate.
10. Next, add page rules to your domain by clicking **Page Rules:**

   (i)   If the URL matches http://example.com/*, then the settings should be Always Use HTTPS.

   (ii) If the URL matches https://example.com/*, then the settings should be Automatic HTTPS Rewrites: ON, and

   (iii) If the URL matches www.example.com/* then the settings should be Forwarding

URL (301 - Permanent Redirect), https://example.com/*.

When you are through with CloudFlare, go to your WordPress, search, install and activate the **Search and Replace** plugin then use it to move all old URLs on your blog from http to https (if any).

How to Back Up Your Blog

You can download your WordPress contents including posts and pages and store them as an XML file as a backup which can be imported into your blog on a later date should the need arises.

For a full backup of your WordPress blog, you can install a WordPress backup plugin, e.g., My WP Backup or other WordPress backup plugins.

To implement a simple WordPress backup, hover your mouse on **Tools** from the **WordPress menu,** and then click on **Export**. On the ensuing page, you can choose to download everything (including posts, pages, contact forms, media files, and ads.txt file (if any)) by selecting **All** or download selected ones only. Finally, click on Download Export File download and store your backup file in XML format. The XML file can be imported into any WordPress blog. See *"Importing Your Old Blogger, WordPress, etc. Blog to Your New WordPress Blog."*

7 ➤ Importing Your Blogger, WordPress, etc. Blog to Your New WordPress Blog

You can merge your old blog parked somewhere with your new WordPress blog and continue from there without losing your comments. This works with blogs from Blogger, Blog roll, LiveJournal, RSS, Movable Type and Type Pad, Tumblr, and WordPress.

To get started, from the **WordPress menu**, hover your mouse on **User Tools** and click on **Import**. Click on the corresponding link to **Install** its plugin. From the installed plugin, connect your account and begin importing your contents to your new WordPress blog.

Once you have your old blog posts in your new WordPress account, reformat them to WordPress standard in the WordPress editor and hit the **Update** button.

8 ➤Understanding Permalinks

Permalinks show how your blog URLs appear. Each URL structure would have a direct impact on your ranking because Google bots also check post URLs to get an idea of what the blog is all about. We will look at these structures shortly. To access your **Permalinks Settings**, hover your mouse on **Settings** from your **WordPress dashboard**, and then click on **Permalinks**. On the **Settings** page, you can see that WordPress can form your blog URL by combining certain parameters.

Plain

Your URL structure here appears common and does not tell anything about the blog post, e.g., http://example.com/?p=123. This is not recommended.

Day and name

Your URL structure here is formed from the date you made your post and the name or title of your blog post, e.g., http://example.com/2019/06/07/sample-post/. This structure looks good but not recommended because of the date being redundant in the URL.

Month and name

Your URL structure here shows the month and year you made your post and the name or title of the post, e.g., http://example.com/2019/06/07/sample-post/. Again, this structure isn't recommended.

Numeric

The URL structure here also appears as the first one. The URL is formed using "archives" plus an auto-generated number. Again, it doesn't tell anything about the post, and hence, not too useful.

Post name

Your URL structure here is formed from the SEO title of your blog post, e.g., http://example.com/WordPress-seo-in-four-steps. This structure appears to be search engine friendly containing no much detail but just your root domain and your SEO title. It is highly recommended because it carries just your SEO title and no redundant text. Google bot can easily understand your blog post. You should go with this option by clicking on the **radio button** against it. Once selected, scroll down and click on **Save Changes**.

9 ➤How to Set Up WordPress Cache

Caching makes your website runs faster and reduces load time for repeated users. A plugin is required to handle your WordPress caching need. Head over to the add plugin page by hovering your mouse on **Plugin** and then **Add New** to download and activate a caching plugin for your blog. A typical cache plugin is the **WP Super Cache**. Type the keyword into the space provided. From the result, locate and install the plugin.

To activate, go to the plugin's admin page or hover your mouse on **Settings** on the left panel to reveal its menu and then clicking **WP Super Cache**. Turn on **Caching** by clicking **Caching On**. Click on **Update Status** to save changes.

You can walk around the tabs to adjust other settings as you wish.

10 ➤ Choosing a Profitable Blogging Idea/Niche

When it comes to blogging for profit, choosing a niche is a different ball game. There are two categories of bloggers on the World Wide Web, those that blog for passion—passion bloggers and those that blog for profit—business bloggers. We belong to the latter category.

Passion bloggers blogs about what they love; they write about things that make them happy. They attend to their blog when they are free to do so. They don't blog necessarily for profit but may want to explore how they can monetize their blog whenever the blog becomes successful.

Business bloggers, on the other hand, blogs for profit, and they work on it to make it a real business they can depend on to pay their bills and take are of other things. This is our approach in this book: building a blog that you can depend on for your daily needs. In building a profitable blog, your choice of a niche would greatly influence how profitable your blog would be in the nearest future. Depending on your choice, some niches take a little longer for organic traffic to build up while others take a shorter time.

Find below some recommended profitable blog niches that you can build a blog around today. Note that this list is not exhaustible. If you cannot choose from the list, feel free to come up with your own blogging idea or niche.

Entertainment

Don't get it wrong, the entertainment niche is a very profitable blog niche, but you'd have to work extra hard to keep your readers satisfied and make them come back to read fresh contents. Every day, people go online to search for fresh or trending entertainment contents. Such covers news about celebrities, song releases (audio and video), hilarious contents (including video clips), latest movie and reviews, etc. To make readers get addicted to your blog, you must be able to post fresh and timely contents, and within a short time, you'd see your traffic building up.

Quotes

You never thought of this, right? Well, quote is one niche that commands thousands of views every month. People search for quotes about a lot of things, e.g., quotes about inspiration, love, life, motivation, depression, being happy, family, sadness, relationship, birthday, change, etc. You can use Google Suggest built into your browser (notably Firefox and Chrome) to generate more than a hundred topic ideas immediately to start with. A simple formula is doing something like: quotes about a, quotes about b, quotes about c, ... quotes about z, and then quotes about ab, quote about ac, and so on. You can't just lack what to write about in this niche.

Bible Verses

Bible verses are a sub-niche within the Christian religious niche. Again, competition is low here, and you can also generate hundreds of high search keywords with low competition. You can also use Google Suggest integrated with the Firefox or Chrome browser to come up with new topics or keywords. While your direct method may be like: Bible verses about a, Bible verses about b, Bible verses about c, etc. to generate keywords, you can also use verses for..., verses about..., verses on... or Bible passages about... to dodge competition albeit with reasonable search volumes.

Bible verses being the Word of God are an evergreen niche. While some post or keywords on an entertainment blog may drop in value or outrightly become useless with time and not fetching in organic traffic again, Bible verses are evergreen. God's Word is fresh every day; people search for Bible verses every day. Hence, it is better to blog in a niche that would always bring in traffic even when you stop posting, but sadly, organic traffic here may not pick up faster like the entertainment niche.

Politics / News

Everybody wants to know what's going on around them. They want to know what's happening in government and society at large. You can feed them with the news. Traffic is high, but news articles drop in value pretty fast. Your news blog may begin to die the day you stop posting contents to it.

Technology How-To / Review

Technology is broad, and this is why I'm specifying where you should stay. People are buying new gears or gadgets every day but don't know how to use them. You can come in to fill the gap. You can also venture into home automation devices. Review and write about them. There's high traffic there.

Natural or Nature's Health

This is not mainstream health but a sub-niche where you can teach people how to take care of their health naturally. People seem to be tired of processed drugs with many side effects. If this is something you feel you can do, you'd have loyal readers over time and they would be ready to patronize whatever you introduce to them.

Making Money Online

Making money online is the passion of most youths around the world. They want to go with their business anywhere they go to. There is high traffic here, but competition is also high. However, with the right keyword research, you can always beat the competition and still rank your blog on Google's first page. Pick a method, do your keyword research to know what people are searching for then craft your article. Once you've exhausted writing about a method, go ahead and pick another method.

Book / e-Reader Reviews

Maybe you don't like reading, a lot of people do. You can read, review, and sell book summaries on your blog. Many want to read as many books as possible within a time frame, but they can't because of other life engagements. I will prefer a good summary book to get an overview of what the actual book talks about. I may stop there or pick up the main text if I wish.

There are millions of readers the world over. That's an opportunity for you.

Auto

The auto niche is another goldmine. You can simply focus on writing about the latest models in town. Get your information right and deliver a quality review. There's high traffic there as well.

Pet

I love pets, and most people do. From food, care, training, behavior, etc., write about everything. Post video of what you do with your pet or what you train them to do and upload on YouTube then link back to your blog. This is one niche you have to blog about passionately if you feel this is what you feel you can handle successfully.

CV and Cover Letter samples

The world's population is exploding, and many job seekers feel the problem is their CV. Who knows? Their CV may be the problem! So they search the web daily looking for targeted CV structure for their job. You can step in to fill this gap while coloring your site with pieces of advice on winning a job and career in general.

Pitching your blog here can be quite profitable as the niche records low competition. There are many kinds of jobs out there. Find out and provide a sample of CV for each one to your readers. You can also position yourself to write CVs and cover letter for people visiting your site. Find out how others are charging for this service and set your fees a little above or below that.

It's over eleven niches there for you. I picked them strategically for your profiting. Pick any one that resonates with you, and build a profitable blog around it.

11 ➤ How to Research for a Profitable Keyword

Attracting organic traffic to your blog is one area that usually frustrates people coming into blogging. For me, I like taking things slowly; I like targeting keywords with low competition. Such keywords/blog posts don't attract much traffic, but with time, they build up and deliver to your site massive and steady traffic stats per day. Remember, a successful blog is a function of time and commitment of the blogger. Hence, don't be in a hurry. Slowly, but surely, you will get there. Growing blog traffic needs time, except you have money to run ad campaigns with Google or Facebook. Don't go writing on a keyword with high competition, you can do that later, but starting now, focus on low competition keywords.

To implement this nature of keyword research to gather organic traffic to your blog, go for keywords with a search volume of 250 and above with a competition between 0.01-0.08 using the Keywords Everywhere add-on (works best on Chrome) to determine [but that's not all]. The golden keyword ratio shouldn't be higher than 0.25.

To get started with this:

1. Download and install the Google Chrome browser on your PC.

2. Download and install on your Chrome browser the "Keyword Everywhere" add-on. Requires no sign-in.

3. Download and install on your Chrome browser the "MozBar" add-on. Sign up and log in.

These are three things that you need to do good keyword research for your new topics. After installation, enable them. Now, throw a seed keyword into the Google search bar. For example, let's try "giving." From the Keyword Everywhere panel by the right-hand side of the screen, we can narrow down to "benefits of giving" with a search volume of 880 per month and 0.01 competition. But that's not all. Search for "benefits of giving," fetches over 562,000,000 results including for topics not necessarily about "benefits of giving," but related to or including the keyword. To filter or weed out some results that are not much a problem, we'd add "AllInTitle:" in front of the keyword before searching Google for the keyword again, i.e., typing "AllInTitle: benefits of giving" into the Google search bar **without the quotations**. With this, the search result drops to 8,320. Dividing "AllInTitle" (numerator) result of a keyword with the "Without AllInTitle" (denominator) result of a keyword gives the keyword ratio figure which determines on **one part** whether you should go for this keyword (if the ratio is <0.25) or move on to another research. For our example here, the keyword ratio is 0.00 [i.e. 8,320/562,000,000] showing a green light on one part.

On the other hand, using the MozBar to analyze the first ten search results on the Google front page where you want your keyword/blog post to show within. We realize that ONLY one result out of the ten passed the Moz test. What's the Moz test all about?

The Moz test strongly suggests that to rank on the first page of Google for your keyword; the first ten search results must contain at least two search results with Page (PA) and Domain Authority (DA) less than or equal to 30 with fewer external links. These weak links or search results are those you target to replace. As said earlier, once a search result meets these criteria, you are good to go. This shows that the difficulty level to rank on the first page of Google for this keyword is high even though the initial analysis favored it.

Notwithstanding, you can still push further by analyzing each of the search results.

1. Check to see if they used the keyword in the title and body of the post, especially in the short first paragraph and if the keyword phrase appears up to five times or more in the blog post. If no, take advantage.

2. Check if sites ranking with this keyword have a mix of multimedia in their blog posts, e.g., video, audio, and images. If no, do a video and/or audio for your new post on this keyword and also use up to three images or more within the body of the

post setting their **alt attribute** with the focus keyword.

3. Check their word counts. Is it up to 1,000? If yes, make yours up to 2,000. Also, use a long tail version of the keyword in the blog post. For example, instead of you to keep using "benefits of giving," you can stretch it to "10 benefits of giving ...in the Bible, ...to your pastor, ...to the poor, etc." <u>Note</u>: Don't try to re-write posts you find on Google. Come up with super fresh contents. This is why it is essential that you pitch your blog where you have an advantage of crafting your articles from your experience or knowledge of the subject. I don't encourage merely re-writing other people's contents without improving on what's already there. Search engines want to see new or unique content.

4. Use more related words or phrases to your main keyword. In our example here, we can use words such as

blessing, love, compassion, kindness, etc. instead of riding with "giving" everywhere in the post.

With this method of keyword research, you focus on keywords with less competition and with time, these little traffic stats on each post would add up to something big. You should aim at writing up to 150-200 highly targeted blog posts before you begin to complain that you are not seeing traffic. Trust me; the result would amaze you.

You can also use Neil Patel's UberSuggest.com or NeilPatel.com site to research for low competition keywords. Go for keywords with SEO Difficulty equal to or lower than 10.

12 ➤ How to Write and Rank on Google and other Search Engines

You are not just going to be writing for humans but considering the major Search Engines (SEs) that most people use to conduct searches online. This nature of writing is different from your usual creative writing. In blogging, we refer to this nature of writing as technical writing. You must carry along both humans and search engine bots in this nature of writing. On the internet today, Google is the No. 1 search engine to consider.

Google records more searches than other SEs, meaning that more people use Google to search for stuff online than they use other SEs, but all searches using these engines follows the same pattern. Obviously, writing for Google is much more the same as writing for other SEs. Focus to get it right with Google and others would fall in place.

Essentially, there are some parameters your article or blog post must satisfy to stand a chance of ranking on Google. These include word count, paragraphing, keyword density, heading style, sentence length, etc. Let's take a look at them one after the other.

In SEO, your focus keyword is the most important SEO element of your blog. It is what tells SEs what your post is all about and if such blog post should form part of the Search Engine Result Page. How you handle it will determine if your blog can rank for it or not.

Your focus keyword should appear in your SEO title

You blog post titles should be what people are searching for on Google and not what you feel it should be if you are blogging for profit. Essentially, every title must be vetted through keyword research before you can settle to craft an article around them. No title should come from your head. If they have to come, they must ultimately align with what people are searching for that keyword.

SEO titles must be validated through a keyword research action. If you just sit and write about what enters your head at any particular time, your posts would never rank on Google first page.

After validating a title through a keyword research action, you must use it as is in your title. For example, if the keyword, "benefits of forgiveness" is your focus keyword, then in your title box, you should have the keyword as is without putting anything in between even if they sound good to be there, e.g., "benefits of giving forgiveness" instead of "benefits of forgiveness." You may wish to add a quantifier; Google loves it, go ahead, e.g., "5 benefits of forgiveness" but don't break the focus keyword.

Keep your SEO title within 50 characters

Google displays up to 50 characters of your SEO title and truncates the rest. As much as you can, keep your title within this length.

Make sure your focus keyword appears in your meta description

Your meta description is your article's excerpts and usually your first few lines by default. Making your focus keyword to appear there naturally can strengthen your blog post to rank on Google for that keyword.

You can also locate an excerpt box by the right side of your WordPress editor when in Block mode or using your SEO plugin, e.g., Yoast, Rank Math, etc.

Make sure your focus keyword appears in your post permalink or URL

This point is crucial when it comes to ranking your post on any search engine. Set your blog to form the article's URL from the blog title. See *"Understanding Permalinks"* to learn more.

What happens is that when people conduct searches, the SEs searches post headers to determine posts that are more relevant to the search query based on searchable keywords use in the blog title. You will miss so much on traffic if your SEO title does not appear in your blog URL.

Make sure your focus keyword to appear in the first paragraph of your blog post

As said earlier, how you use your focus keyword tells Google how relevant the keyword is with respect to the content of your blog post. Many bloggers feel it's about repeating the focus keyword in the blog post as many times as possible. No! It's rather about using them strategically or intelligently. Google can penalize your blog if it detects that you are stuffing keyword to gain undue advantage.

There are key places your focus keyword should appear in your post, and once you can place them there, you are good to go.

We'll come back to this later, but right now, make your focus keyword appear in the first paragraph of your post which should be kept short. The keyword must flow naturally.

Use your focus keyword in your blog content

Here, we are talking about the keyword density — a measure of how many times your focus keyword appears in your post. There is no specific number of times you should make your primary keyword to appear in your blog post, but the key thing is to make it appear natural.

You can turn your readers off if you use them unintelligently. One formula to make it appear many times and naturally in your blog post is to write long contents; meaning that the more you write, the more you use the primary keyword but this time in its long tail form (if any).

Content length as a ranking factor

Google also considers content length in ranking a blog post. As it is believed that more book pages equate to more value, so is Google also thing long content carries more information or value about a subject. Here, I'm not saying that short contents don't rank, but once it ranks, it stays there. You can't just outrank it.

For a new blog, content length matters a lot and to successfully compete with the old blogs that are deeply rooted on the web, you must write better — in content length, quality, formatting, rich content (multimedia), rich snippet (rating system), etc. Write exhaustively.

Where you don't have much to write about, the content length should be at least 700-1,000 words and where words flow freely, take your post up to 2,000-3,000 word length or even more. More importantly, consider word counts of other blogs ranking on the same keyword.

Maintain short URLs

Your URL largely depends on your SEO title. That means you should keep your SEO title short — containing basically the focus keyword and bringing other things later. Google can only show up to 70 characters of your URL and truncate the rest.

On the results page, searchers mostly look at a site's URL and the excerpts that show and once they see that it addresses what they are looking for, they click on it. This is why you must try as much as you can to maintain short URLs [and SEO title] that shows everything.

Make sure your focus keyword to appear in the sub-headings such as H2, H3, etc.

Making your focus keyword to appear in your sub-heading further reinforce the keyword on SEs. See to it that your focus keyword appears in the sub-heading even once to further strengthen the intent of the whole blog post. SEs also read blog post sub-headings to see how much the post talks about the focus keyword of the article, which further establishes the relevance of the entire blog post.

Optimized your Featured Image

Every WordPress blog editor has a provision for featured image. Use it. Upload a clear image that relates to your blog content. Make sure you fill the box for alt attribute with the post's focus keyword. This would help in Google image search result. Remember, Google also displays relevant images tight to the keyword in question.

Inject external links into your blog post

Don't stop at just writing a blog post, catch up on searchers that searches for "focus keyword + pdf," e.g., "benefits of forgiveness pdf." Many times, searchers want to enrich their e-readers with contents they can always refer back to and not have to load a webpage again. On this note, you can take a little time and work out a downloadable format of the same blog post, upload it somewhere and drop a link of the download on your post. (e.g., "Download available: benefits of forgiveness pdf"). File download sites you can explore include Google Drive, Mediafire, OneDrive, Mega Cloud, Yandex, orDropbox for all your media uploads then pick thedownload link and use on your blog.

To make it clearer, using Google Drive as an example;

- Launch Google Drive from your Gmail.

- Click on New then upload file.

- Pick up the blog post on your system in pdf format.

- After a successful update, click on the file and get the shareable link. Permit anyone with a link to view the file.

- Copy the link to your WordPress editor, select the text you want to wrap the link on, e.g., "Download: 5 benefits of forgiveness pdf." When you select a text and wrap it with a link, the area you selected appears underlined, and if anyone clicks the underlined area it takes the person to the download page of the file.

- Using any other file upload service to upload your pdf$_s$ follows a similar process.

Add DoFollow links to your blog post

There's nothing wrong with linking to a similar blog post in another blog or website. Doing that validates your content and help readers to gain more knowledge about the subject. However, you must link out to a standard site and not some crappy website.

Keyword density

Keyword density is basically a measure of the number of times a focus keyword appears in a blog post. We've discussed this before, but the point remains that there's no ideal figure. Make them flow naturally as it should be. Make your content long to use more keywords within it. Long contents can accommodate up to 10 times.

To add more to this, collect synonyms or related words to your focus keyword and also use in the content. For our example here on "5 benefits of forgiveness," you can incorporate words or phrases such as letting go, embracing peace, let go, move on, peace, holding grudges, offense, etc. into the content.

Add links to other contents within the blog

Here, we are talking about internal links. Sure, you have related blog post to the one you are creating, bring them in — three or four should be fine. Even if they are not related, you can still bring them in as far as they are on the same blog.

To link internally to other blog posts, visit your blog using another tab, open the blog post that you want to link to and copy its URL. Go back to your content at hand and do something like: "READ ALSO: Why you should forgive today." Position your internal links strategically where they are relevant after a paragraph.

Write quantified articles

For whatever reason, SEs, especially Google, loves quantified articles. Except not possible or applicable, use list; write list articles. By list, I mean arranging thoughts within your post using a bulleted list, especially at the beginning of the article. For example, "5 benefits of forgiveness," instead of "benefits of forgiveness" and then arranging those "benefits" within the article using bulleted points.

Arrange your thoughts using a table of contents

It's not only when writing a book that you should use a table of contents, you can use it to lay out you post. Using our example here for "5 benefits of forgiveness," you can draw up a simple table of contents for this title. Let's see:

- What is forgiveness?

- What does the Bible say about forgiveness?

- 5 benefits of forgiveness.

- Final thoughts.

- More resources.

That's it! Simple and straight; addressing the subject and Google loves it too. Going forward, install, and activate the **Easy Table of Content** plugin for this.

Add multimedia to your blog post

Images, GIFs, audio, and video makes blog content looks richer and can help it rank better on SEs. If you are challenged by storage space, upload your videos to YouTube and link (embed) to them from your blog. See *"Adding an Image, Audio, or Video into a WordPress post"* to learn more.

13 ➤ Creating a Navigational Menu in WordPress

Navigational menus would help your blog readers to walk around your blog with ease. Linking up a blog post to the navigational menu follows a hierarchy. First, a blog post is linked to a category, and the category is linked to the menu. A category, page, post, link, etc. can also be placed on a navigational menu bar.

To create a navigational menu, hover your mouse on **Appearance** from the **WordPress menu** (left panel) and click on **Menus**. On the Menus page, we have two tabs, **Edit Menu** and **Manage Locations.**

Edit Menu

Under this tab, you can either edit an existing menu or create a new menu. Now, click on **Create A Menu** and enter a name for it in the box provided, e.g., menu 1, and then click on **Create Menu**. On the left side of the screen, you have items placed in their categories that you can add to the menu you've just created.

These include items from Pages, Products (if any), Custom Links, Categories, Product Categories (if any), etc. For instance, to add items under **Pages**, click on **View All** and start by clicking on the checkbox against the items that you want to add to the main menu, e.g., Home, Contact, About Us, etc. Once you are done selecting them, click on **Add to Menu**. Shortly, the items are added to the menu structure by right.

Try to click other categories by the left to see how they open up to reveal their contents that you can also add to the main menu. Most times, the menu bar is made up of items from Pages and Categories. At any time that you create a new page or category and wish to add it to the navigational menu bar, you can always repeat the same process as explained here. As a rule, try to create your pages and categories that you want to be part of your navigational menus before coming to the Menus screen.

To add a custom link, click on it and enter a URL and a **Link Text** in the text box and then click on **Add to Menu** to add the link to the navigational menu. Once you are done building your menu, click on **Save Menu** to save your changes.

Manage Locations

On this tab, click on the **Navigation Menu**, click the box and select your main navigational menu. In our case here, select **Menu 1** from the dropdown. Remember when we created it? Oh yes! Finally, click on **Save Changes**. Head over to your site now and refresh the page. See what we've got? Well, you did it!

Does it end there? No! You can do more like rearranging the menu items or making one a child and the other a parent to create a main and sub-menu.

Now, go back to the menu screen by hovering your mouse on **Appearance** and then clicking **Menus**. Under the **Menu Structure,** click and hold an item; drag it up or down to re-arrange or try to indent it (push it a little to the right) to make it a child or a sub-menu over or under the item just above it.

Finally, click on **Save Menu** to save the new changes you've just made.

In essence, you can have sub-menus or sub-categories under the main menu or category. You can also have multiple sub-categories or sub-sub-categories for the main menu, but first you'd have to arrange or create a sub-menu or category and then sub-sub-menu or categories and so on. It's up to you.

See example below:

Home

Blog

Breaking News

Tech

Entertainment

Audio

Video

Where;

- Home and Blog are your main navigational menus.

- Breaking News, Tech, and Entertainment are your sub menus under Blog; and

- Audio and Video are your sub-sub-menu or categories under Entertainment.

To customize the individual menu items, click on the little arrow ▼ against the menu item that you want to customize to see options about the item. From there, you can change the Navigation Label, Title Attribute, etc. Click on the small arrow again when you are through. You can also **Cancel** the changes you've made or completely **Remove** the item from the menu structure by clicking the appropriate link. Finally, click on **Save Menu** to save changes.

To see the changes that you are making in real time, click on **Manage in Customizer** or **Manage in Live Preview** depending on WordPress version. From there, as you adjust the menu location you will also see the new changes immediately in the live preview. Finally, click on **Save and Publish** to save and publish your changes.

14 ➤ Category and Tags

A category defines your blog post classification. Most likely, you will need to create categories for your blog posts to help organize your contents for easy navigation. For instance, if you are running a gospel music blog, category options for your gospel music uploads may include praises, worships, hymns, acapella, etc.

Categories and your navigational menu work together; where categories can be seen as items in a basket, the navigational menu can be seen as the basket that holds the items. If you don't link your categories to a menu, they'd just float there.

Tags can be used in place of categories, but categories can't be used in place in tags.

Let's look at the illustration below:

Category A	Category B	Category C
Post 1	Post 1	Post 1
Post 2	Post 3	Post 3
Post 4	Post 5	Post 4
Post 6	Post 6	Post 7

Tag A	Tag B	Tag C
Post 1	Post 1	Post 1
Post 2	Post 3	Post 3
Post 4	Post 5	Post 4
Post 6	Post 6	Post 7

The illustration above shows that you can have a post in one or more categories, and you can also use a tag in one or more blog posts. Therefore, it means that you can use a tag to replace a category, but you can't use a category to replace a tag. However, to place a tag under a menu, you will need to get the URL of the tag and create the menu as a **custom link** via **Appearance>Menus**. It's now a question of which is better to use. Well, as far as Search Engines can crawl either of the two links, you can go with any, but for convenience, go with category to create your navigational menu and still use tags to bind related posts together.

You can create a category to link your blog post to it within the WordPress editor. To create a category in the WordPress editor, locate the category block by the right panel and click on the little arrow to open it up and then click **Add New Category**. Give it a name and then click **Add New Category** to add the new category as a parent category. You can also choose a category from the drop down to make the new category that you are creating a child to the selected one or as a sub-menu to it.

Tick any **checkbox** against a category name to assign the post you are creating to that category. Don't forget that you can add your post to more than one category. Finally, click **Publish** or **Update** as the case may be to publish your changes. When a category is selected or clicked from the navigational menu, all blog posts linked to it are shown on the screen.

A little down the WordPress editor screen, just after the category block is the tag box, enter a tag to link the current post to it. You can also choose from existing tags. In naming a tag, you can use a word or short phrase. Finally, click **Publish** or **Update** as the case may be to publish your changes. When a tag is selected from the tag cloud or just below a blog post that you find it, all blog posts sharing that tag are shown on the screen, and the tag URL is shown in the address bar.

How to manage your categories and tags

To manage your categories, hover your mouse on **Posts** from the **WordPress menu** by left and then click on **Categories**. From there, you can also create a new category by typing the category name using the **Name** box. You may choose to enter a word or phrase for the slug. Select the category level (parent or child to another category) and write a description for it (optional). Finally, click on **Add New Category**.

By the right of the screen, you have all your categories listed there; you can edit or delete a category(s) from there. To try, move your mouse over your category of interest and click **Edit**, **Quick Edit, Delete** or **View** as the case may be. If editing, don't forget to click **Update** to save your changes after you've edited the category. To delete more than one category at once, mark the category and then click on **Bulk Actions**, select **Delete** and finally, click **Apply** to delete the selected categories.

Similarly, you can also hover your mouse on **Posts** and then click on **Tags** to manage your tags. The process is similar.

How to Convert Categories to Tag and Vice-Versa

You can convert your categories to tags and vice-versa with the help of the Categories to Tags Converter. To get started, from the

WordPress menu, hover your mouse on **Tools** and click on **Available Tools**.

On the ensuing page, locate and click on **Categories to Tags Converter** and then click on **Install Now** from the Import page. Click **Run Importer** when the installation is completed.

At the top of the page are two link buttons: **Categories to Tags** and **Tags to Categories**. Click on any to see the items that are related to it. From the list, use the checkboxes to select the categories or tags that you want to convert to the other.

Finally, click the corresponding button down the page to do the conversion.

15 ➤ Adding and Setting up Widgets

Widgets are link boxes you find on a WordPress blog. They can be added by the left or right side of the blog depending on the Theme. To go to the widgets page, hover your mouse on **Appearance** and then click on **Widgets**. On the widgets page, we have **Available Widgets** by the left and **sidebar** by right. Generally, your widgets and its arrangement would depend on your blog theme.

To start creating or setting up widgets, click, drag and drop a widget item from the **Available Widgets** to the sidebars based on your **Theme Settings** for widgets. You will find options to set up a widget for your Home page sidebar, header ad, and footer widgets. Customize your widget as you wish where necessary.

16 ➤The WordPress Editor

The WordPress Editor, just like any other text editor, is your workspace for typing and formatting your blog post before publishing it. However, it is recommended that you type your blog post elsewhere, e.g., Microsoft Word and then copy and paste the text using the paste icon in your WordPress editor. If you type using the WordPress editor, your WordPress online session may expire before you finish typing the post.

To get started when in **Classic Mode**, enter the title of your post in the **Add Title** box. Highlight, copy, and paste your text into the workspace. You may wish to type it there, it's up to you. o what formatting features are essential?

There are over six levels of headings (Heading 1 - 6) in the WordPress editor. We also have other formatting features such as the font type, font size, etc. There are all there for you to explore and exploit, depending on your blog post. Let's assume you've pasted a text into the editor with paragraphs and headings in it.

To start formatting, highlight your introductory heading (if any), click where you have **Paragraph** to see other styles, from the dropdown, click on **Heading 1**. You've just made a line of text a main heading. Depending on the heading styles you want subsequent headings to take, you can select Heading 2 which falls directly under Heading 1, while Heading 3 falls under 2 and so on. You can keep the font size of your headings at 18 or 24.

Once you've taken care of your headings, you can highlight and format other text as **Paragraph**.

Other formatting features that may be of interest to you are listed below. To use any, highlight the section of the text you want the formatting to affect.

- Make a text bold by clicking B

- Italicize a text by clicking *I*

- Create a blockquote by clicking "

- Create a bulleted list by clicking
- Create a numbered list by clicking
- Align your text left, center or right
- Paste a text as a plain text by clicking
- Insert a link by clicking
- Remove a link by clicking
- Undo your last action by clicking
- Redo your last action by clicking
- Decrease your indent by clicking
- Increase your indent by clicking
- Clear formatting on a text by clicking
- Insert special characters by clicking
- Insert read more tag by clicking
- Color your text by clicking
- Insert a table in your post by clicking

Note: Always highlight or select the area you want to apply a formatting before clicking on the formatting feature.

17 ➤ Creating Links in Your WordPress Post

Internal links within a blog post are meant to engage your blog readers on your site more and more while external links are meant to point them to external resources apart from those on your blog. Generally, links can help your blog rank better on Search Engines.

You must have seen or come across some links wrapped on a text such that if you click on the text/link, you are taken to a new webpage which may be within the same tab or webpage, or a completely new tab or webpage. While some links still point to the same domain or website that you are working on (internal links), others take you to a different site (external links).

The point is that you can easily copy and paste a link into your block, but that's not a standard practice, it doesn't look clean, so you'd have to wrap all your links on a text or image while the text or image tells what the link is all about [and encouraging users to click on it].

To create a link in your WordPress post, highlight a portion of a text click on an image within the post that you want to hold the link and then click the **Insert Link** icon, enter or paste the link into the box provided and hit the **Save Link** icon or the **Enter** button on your Computer keyboard. To remove a link from a text, highlight the text and click on the **Remove Link**icon .

18 ➤ Adding an Image, Audio or Video into a WordPress Post

Multimedia, apart from adding beauty to a blog post can also help your blog reader to understand better what a post is all about. Multi-media also contribute positively to search engine optimization.

Adding any kind of multimedia (image, audio or video) into a WordPress post is made possible with the **Add Media** button **Add Media** which can be found just below the title box. To add any kind of multimedia, place your mouse where you want the media file to be and then click on the **Add Media** button. On your **Media Library**, there are two tabs: one to **Upload** your media files from your Computer and the other to add a media file to your post from your blog's **Media Library**.

If you've not uploaded the media file that you want to add to your post, click on the **Upload Files** tab and then **Select Files**. On your Computer, browse to where the media file is located, select and double-click on it. Wait for the media file to finish uploading and then (type the focus keyword of your post into the **Alt Text** box if it is an image file, scroll down and tune the **Attachment Display Settings**). Finally, click on **Insert Into Post** (if it's an image file) or **Embed Into Post** (if it's an audio or video media file) to see the media file in your post.

To insert a media file into your post from the **Media Library** tab, select the file and click on **Insert/Embed Into Post** as the case may be for an image, audio/video file. If you have lots of media files uploaded to your media library, you can filter what you want to see by clicking **All Media Items**. From the drop down, make your choice to see related media files. Don't forget to add an Alt Text to your image files before inserting them into your WordPress post.

Generally, to manage your media files, hover your mouse on the **Media** button from the **WordPress menu** by the left side of the screen and click on **Library.** In the Media Library, you can find all your media files all parked together and shown on the page. Use the **All Media Items** and **All**

Dates menus to filter the media files by **types** and **dates** they were uploaded to the library. You can also search for a specific media file using the **search box**.

Once you click on a file in the library, e.g., an image file, you can delete the file permanently by clicking **Delete Permanently**. Click on the **Edit More Details** link to set the image's **Alternative Text** and then **Update** to save your changes to the image file.

To add more media files to the library, click on the **Add New** button and then **Select Files** to select and upload the media file from your Computer. You can upload more than one media file at a time.

19 ➤Creating, Editing or Deleting a WordPress Post

So you are set to make your first post in WordPress? Make it fast then. From the **WordPress Dashboard**, move your mouse over **Posts** and then click on **Add New**. From there, you are taken to the WordPress Editor. Click on the **Add Title** box to enter your post title. Proceed to the Wordpress workspace to start typing from your blog post or copy and paste your text from the MS-Word or any other text editor.

When you are through with that, locate the **Publish** button on the right panel and hit it to make your blog post go live. You've just made your first post in WordPress.

You can edit your post immediately and then click on **Update** to publish those new changes. You can only publish your post once and then keep updating.

To edit/update your post on a later date, hover your mouse on **Posts** and then click **All Posts**. Locate the post you want to edit/update from the list, move your mouse over it to see the options that associate with it, click **Edit**. Edit the post from the editor and then click **Update** to post your changes.

To delete or move a post to the recycle bin, move your mouse over the post and click **Trash**. To delete more than a post, click the small box against the post you want to trash, now, go back to where you have **Bulk Actions** and click on it. From the dropdown, select **Move to Trash**. Finally, click on **Apply** just beside **Bulk Actions** to delete the post.

You can use **All Dates**, **All Categories** and **All Posts** menus to filter your content, once you set an option, click on **Filter**.

Navigate through the pages of your posts using the navigational buttons (see top or bottom right side of the All Posts screen).

20 ➤Creating, Editing or Deleting a WordPress Page

To create your first page in WordPress, from the WordPress Dashboard, move your mouse over **Pages** and then click on **Add New**. From there, you are taken the WordPress Editor for Pages. Click on the **Add Title** box to enter your page title and then proceed to the Wordpress workspace to start typing your post text. Alternatively, copy and paste your text from the MS-Word or any other text editor. After typing, locate the **Publish** button on the right panel and click on it to publish your page.

You can also save the page as a draft if you don't want to publish it immediately by clicking **Save Draft**. Set a **Featured Image** for your page by clicking **Set Featured Image** under **Featured Image**. You've just created your first page in WordPress.

You can edit your page immediately and click on **Update** to publish changes. Like your usual blog post, you can only publish your page once and then keep updating. To edit/update your page on a later date, hover your mouse on **Pages** and then click **All Pages**. Locate the page that you want to edit/update from the list, move your mouse over it to see the options that associate with it, click **Edit**. Edit the page from the editor and then click **Update** to publish your changes.

To delete or move a page to the recycle bin, move your mouse over the page and click **Trash**. To delete more than a post, click the small box against the page you want to trash, now, go back to where you have **Bulk Actions** and click on it. From the dropdown, select **Move to Trash**.

Use the **All Dates**, and **All Posts** menus to filter your pages, once you set an option, click on **Filter**. Navigate through the pages of your posts using the navigational buttons (see the top or bottom right side of the All Pages screen).

You can also add a new page from this screen by clicking on the **Add New** button (see top left side of the All Pages screen).

21 ➤ Add Your Sitemap and Analyze Your Google Search Performance with Google Search Console

The Google Search Console (GSC) is a free tool from Google that webmasters can use to see how their site is doing in Google Search Engine. We also have the Bing Webmaster Tool for Yahoo Search Engine.

Essentially, the GSC is meant to help Google to discover your contents and also to show you how your site is performing on Google. With the Google Webmaster Tool, you can:

(1.) Understand what Googlebot couldn't crawl on your site.

(2.) Test your sitemap file and submit same to Google.

(3.) Generate or analyze robots.txt files.

(4.) Set your preferred domain and links to be crawled by Googlebot.

(5.)   Receive and review crawling errors.

To get started with GSC, go to https://search.google.com/ and login with your gmail account and then proceed to add your site by following the steps below.

(a) Click on **Add Property**

Add property   ▾

(b) Enter your domain name under **Domain** tab.

(c) Click **Continue** and copy the code shown.

(d) Visit your domain name registrar and login to see the dashboard where your domain name is listed.

(e) Click **Manage** against your domain name. 6. Go to **Advanced DNS** and under **Host Records**, click on **Add New Record** as **TXT Record** from the drop down menu.

(f) Type @ for host and paste the code you copied from Google under **Value**.

(g) Go back to Google Search Console and click **Verify**.

Congrats! You've just added your site to Google Search Console.

From your WordPress dashboard, add a new plugin called **Simple WP Sitemap** to use in creating your sitemap file. Install and activate the copy and then click on the plugin **Settings**. Copy the XML sitemap link from the **plugin settings** and take it to GSC.

On the Simple WP Sitemap settings, in the **General** tab and under **Add pages**, manually gather and add your WordPress pages that you want to be a part of the sitemap file. You can also add pages that you want Google to exempt from indexing under **Block pages,** e.g., Privacy Policy, Contact Us, About Us, etc. Finally, click on **Save Changes**.

Click on **Sitemaps** by the left and paste the XML sitemap link in the space provided. Finally, click **Submit** to submit your sitemap to Google for indexing of all your blog posts only.

Congrats again! You've just submitted your blog sitemap to GSC for indexing. Going forward, you don't need to submit another sitemap when you update your blog with more posts; Google would take care of that automatically. You can now monitor your keywords that are ranking on Google. Now, you can walk around the site to familiarize yourself with other features of the GSC.

In future, go back to GSC, click on **Sitemap** to see your submitted sitemap and then click on **See Index Coverage** to see your **Coverage**.

22 ➤ Managing Comments on Your Blog

Comments make a website engaging because they allow blog readers to react to the post or communicate with you and other readers. It helps people to say what's in their mind about your post and solve their problems in the process. You can choose to approve or unapprove what a reader post to your blog so there's nothing to worry about. You have total control of all comments on your blog.

On your WordPress dashboard, under **At A Glance**, you can see the number of comments that you have and those awaiting moderation. To see all comments, including those awaiting moderation, click on **Comments** from the WordPress menu by left.

For comments awaiting moderation, move your mouse on any of them to see the options that you can effect on it. Such include not just an option to **Approve** the comment, but you can also **Reply** a comment without leaving the dashboard, **Edit**, mark as **Spam** or **Trash** the comment. After approving a comment to show up on your site, the **Approve** link or button changes to **Unapprove**, that means you can also **Unapprove** an Approved comment to push it off your blog.

Above the comment blog, we have options to see **All** your comments, **Pending** comments, comments that have been **Approved**, those marked as **Spam** as well as comments that have been **Trash**ed. Click on any to see the number of comments that each one hold. You can choose to go to **Spam** and tell WordPress that a particular comment is **Not Spam**. You can also choose to **Delete Permanently** a spam comment. Hover your mouse on any comment inside the **Spam** box to see these options.

Click on Pending to see only comments awaiting your moderation. You can also mark more than a comment and take a **Bulk Action**. Don't forget to click **Apply** after selecting a **Bulk Action.**

It's important to adjust the settings about managing your comments so that some things can be handled automatically. Settings for comments can be found via **Settings>Discussions**. Study the options and tick or untick as appropriate. Scroll down and click **Save Changes** when you are done.

23 ➤ How to Stop Google from Penalizing Your Blog

In most cases, Google can't come directly for your blog even if you are doing some wrong things. What they do is to roll out some updates that would set your blog backward. Hence, whether you depend on Google for blog monetization or not, they practically rule the commercial web and can make your blog suffer if your blog falls under their hammer.

Imagine your site that started ranking and garnering reasonable organic traffic crashing to the bed. Remember, your blog depends on traffic for whatever monetization option you go for. Once your traffic crashes, your earnings also crash. It's better not to rise than to rise and fall.

The fact is that they don't demand much from you or your blog other than doing the right thing. They expect you don't engage in sharp practices aka white/black hat tricks to gain undue advantage. You have a conscience, and any time you are tempted to try any of the things they frown at, you will know. Hence, do your best to keep your blog clean, and with time, you will get to the top.

Generally, Google hates keyword stuffing (unnecessarily repeating keywords within a blog post). Let your focus keywords flow naturally. Don't promote or give a voice to illegal stuff on your blog, e.g., copyright/plagiarism, violence, alcohol, pornography/nudity, smoking, etc.

24 ➤ Actionable Ways to Skyrocket Your Blog Traffic

1. Try as much as you can to use all associated keywords to your focus keyword in your blog post. Don't squeeze more keyword into your primary keyword. Rather, make all related keywords to flow naturally in the blog post. Feel free to also use synonyms, instead of repeating the same word over and over. Collect all related keywords during keyword research and take your time to sprinkle them in the post—no spamming!

2. Open a Facebook group that relates to your niche. Grow the group with meaningful discussions. Share your post link with members of your group intelligently. Don't stop at group, open a Fan page as well and grow it. You will need it if you want to run a traffic campaign.

3. Answer a query on HARO. This can result in referral traffic to your site. It's also a great way of building high-quality inbound links.

4. Reach out to other bloggers in the blogging community such as CopyBlogger or ProBlogger to exchange links and cross-promote contents.

5. Become a contributor on popular websites such as Huffington Post or Forbes. This helps drive targeted traffic to your blog.

6. Trade banner ads with sites within the site niche.

7. Tweet more often using trending hashtags in your blog industry and also mention influencers using @mention in your tweets.

8. Create pages with a long content highlighting top related blog posts on your blog and pin them within the blog.

9. Create short videos and upload them to YouTube. Take the links and embed them in your blog post. Grow your channel using searchable keywords and relevant tags.

10. Respond to comments on your blog. Show that you care. Build a relationship with your readers.

11. Answer questions on Quora and Yahoo! Answers cloaking your links and referring readers to your blog.

12. Organize your post in categories.

13. Comment on popular industry blogs and drive traffic to your blog. Drop relevant links. No spamming.

14. Share your blog excerpts on Facebook.

15. Tell people about your blog.

16. Print a t-shirt with your blog URL on it.

25 ➤ Profiting from Social Media

Every social media influencer started from zero followers to thousands or millions of followers they have today. You can also be counted with time if you put in the effort needed to grow your social media followers and then profit from it.

One lasting method of growing your following is by providing value to your followers and not by using a robot to build up artificial followers that can't convert, but you must also follow others.

Now, start by signing up on your platform of choice and start following others while making a useful post on your page even when you are yet to have a follower. Most times, it is family members and friends that kick-starts a course for people, and you have to leverage on this as well. Talk to your friends and family members and get them to follow, comment, and like your posts. Shortly, the system begins to suggest your handle to others based on your posts and followers, and you keep growing.

Throw offers to your followers, e.g., free eBooks with valuable information and make your page engaging. Don't just scramble for followers on social media but quality ones that would be ready to patronize any offer you put across to them. Keep on posting quality content and adding value to the system. See how you can make a deal with influencers to promote you on the platform.

Encourage your readers to follow you on social media in every blog post that you publish. However, if you want to scale up things, you can run a traffic campaign for your page and target the ad to show only to a relevant audience. While your ultimate intention may be to sell something to your followers, you must also learn to offer them free stuff centered on your niche. With time, you can even do a competition and whoever wins receives a package from the postman.

26 ➤ Building Backlinks

In Search Engine Optimization, backlinks refer to links of your blog post or website URL placed in other websites and pointing to your blog. In simple terms, they are inbound links to your website. It is such that when anybody clicks on them, they end up on your blog. Backlinks, no doubt help in making a blog post ranks well on search engines.

In the past, they used to be applications or services that can send your links to web directories. Maybe that worked then, but right now, if you try that, you'd be doing your blog more harm than good.

The point is that those web directories that your links may be sent to are poor websites; they have no quality and their focus or niche may not be related to your blog niche. In building backlinks, you don't just drop links anywhere; only quality links can help your post to rank better. Generally, Google prohibits porn sites, gambling sites, etc.

Where you should drop your links

- Active websites.

- Better quality websites with high domain authority

- Link to websites in a similar niche like yours.

- Don't link to free blogs.

Search engines, among other things, use links to validate how relevant your content may be and also to pick up new keywords and web pages. Apart from Google favoring your blog as a result of links in other websites pointing to yours, visitors can directly click on those links and get to your site. Hence, link building can lead to a surge in your organic and inorganic traffic. However, you have to do it right to have it makes perfect sense.

There are less and more important links. Less important links don't help in organic traffic or ranking of your links on Google. These are "nofollow" links. "NoFollow" attribute tells Google not to consider the link for ranking.

There are basically no shortcuts to building high-quality links. It's a slow process but may be very rewarding in the long term. Links that get published with the "nofollow" attributes are mostly links from forum posts, blog comments, guest book comments, links from Wikipedia, guest post signatures, Yahoo! Answers, etc. Why are they so? Because it's very easy to post any of these links and they may constitute spams on the websites you are posting them. Remember, others also do the same. Thus, these are not high-quality links, and they can't help rank your blog on Google. They are links with the "nofollow" attribute automatically attached to them. However, they can still bring traffic to your blog depending on the number of people that sees and follow them to your blog.

How then can you build high-quality links? One effective way of going about building high-quality backlinks is guest posting. Guest posting is crafting a long content and approaching a webmaster of a related blog and have them post the content on their site. Such post should be laced with links clothed with a link tag and visible/anchor text (e.g., <a href=https://example.com>This is an anchor text </a>) and pointing to your website. In one guest post, you can lace up to five different blog posts from your blog, but this would depend on the keyword within the guest post. If you make your content long enough, you can have more keywords that you can cloth with links. However, take note that guest posting comes with a cost. Other times, you may not have to do a guest post but simply approaching a Webmaster of your targeted blog and have them cloth your links on relevant keywords on their website.

To discover websites in a similar niche like yours for your link building campaign, you can use a free tool like UberSuggest.com or any other tool that you know. When you get to the site, enter your keyword, and then **Search**. Down the page, you can find websites that have published articles on the keyword. You can contact the admins of those sites for a guest post deal. You can also take another step to take a domain name from the list then click on **Backlinks** under **SEO Analyzer** and insert the domain name to see where that domain is getting their links from. You can also go to those places to get links.

27 ➤ Beyond the Scrambling for Google's SERP

When putting thoughts together to write a blog post for your blog, you have to be very careful not to be seen as someone who's only chasing for traffic and not much interested in adding value. The main essence of a blog is to add value to people's life. Blogs are meant to add to knowledge and stand out as an authority in the industry.

You must strive to build a blog that in ten years from now when you look at your old contents, you will still be proud of yourself. You should be able to ask yourself what special thing you are bringing to the table. This is the only thing that would inspire you to put more effort into the site and make it stand out. If you are coming into blogging with plans of only rewriting other people's content, you may likely fail. This is because most visitors that come to your site have probably visited or opened a similar article from another blog and when they see that the contents are the same, they close your blog's tab immediately and that increases your bounce rate, which is an important parameter that Google uses to rank a site. When your bounce is high, it simply tells Google that your blog isn't relevant so that shouldn't bother to rank it.

Don't say there's nothing new under the sun, come up with a different strategy; add to knowledge from your brain let others learn from you. Let people see your uniqueness in expression or imparting knowledge. That's what would make them come back and keep reading your contents. Some may even convert your blog posts to pdf and store on their devices. Look beyond the profit but developing contents or building a blog that would stand the test of time. One that readers would be eager to refer others to it.

To this end, your contents must be:

- Exhaustive.

- Fresh.

- Aesthetically appealing, i.e., well formatted.

- Linking out to more useful resources.

- Engaging.

- Use simple English — most readers wouldn't want to refer to the dictionary before understanding some of your terms.

- Post to your blog frequently. Have a blogging plan.

28 ➤ 13 Ways to Monetize Your Blog

1. Using advertising networks to display ads on your blog, e.g., **Adsense**, **Mediavine**, etc.

2. Create and sell your products related to your niche, e.g., eBooks, physical products, etc.

3. Promoting affiliate products of big online e-commerce platforms, e.g., **Amazon** via Amazon Associate, **ClickBank**, **ShareASale**, **Commission Junction/CJ**, etc. Other times, you can also search for and work directly with companies related to your niche to promote their products and earn commissions.

4. Reviewing products of big companies related to your blog niche.

5. Selling advertising space on your blog using image widgets to display ads.

6. RSS adverts using **BidVertiser**, **Google FeedBurner**, etc.

7. Let people consult you for services, e.g., $50 per hour to teach about weight loss using Skype.

8. Get hired from your blog: Here, you can make yourself open to readers of your blog to hire you for services to be rendered physically or virtually. Don't forget that this must connect directly to your niche, e.g., if blogging about wedding and related issues; you can ask your readers to hire you for services about any of; wedding invitation card designs, favor cards, preparing slide show presentation for the wedding pictures, managing the event, etc.

9. Offer free and premium content: Depending on your niche or nature of the site, you can decide to offer free and premium content by enabling login to your premium membership area. However, such premium content has to be something that isn't common on the net.

10. Survey and Polls: You can also conduct survey and polls for your website on people or companies seeking to get responses of people about their products or services and get paid for it. This would largely depend on your traffic base.

11. Also, depending on your niche, you can get companies to place adverts for jobs on your website. However, this will depend on your site traffic stats. Wordpress plugins to use for this purpose include, Jobpress, Jobpress Professional, etc.

12. You can also choose to monetize your blog by receiving donations from readers. PayPal comes in handy here for global coverage.

13. Once your website is fully developed, list it to sell on Flippa and then build another one from scratch.

Last Words

Blogging for profit is a big business. It's not a child's play, especially if you want to see results really fast. There are rules to the game, and you must stick to them. Don't rush; take your time and walk through every step.

Soil your hands with the art so that you can fully understand what it's all about. Examine all your investments so that you don't end up wasting money. Don't stop here, read more, and discover more. Put in your best, and you'd see the result, even faster than you imagined.

30562278R00078

Printed in Great
Britain
by Amazon